# Take Pain and Walk

## Collection of Poems

### By Charlise R. Rice

To my mother from whom the title evolved, my son Loron, the love of my life Shaun, and my father. You all are my motivational push.
Thank God for you all being in my life.

All rights reserved. No part of this book may be reproduced in any form or by any electronic or mechanical means including information storage and retrieval systems, without permission in writing from the author. The only exception is a reviewer, who may quote short excerpts in a review. For permissions contact info@lisesbusiness.com

Cover design created with Canva Pro version

Biblical Scriptures are from the New International Version (NIV) and King James Version (KJV). The Holy Bible

Find other books under the pen name
Charlise R. Walker

Books & Merch website https://www.CharliseRice.com
Professional Resource Consultant website
https://www.LisesBusiness.com

Printed in the United States of America
Paperback ISBN 979-8-9879207-1-8
Hardback 979-8-9879207-2-5

Take Pain and Walk: Collection of Poems
Copyright © 2018 Revised 2023 Charlise R. Rice

# CONTENTS

## Love........................................................................................1
To Loron M. Young
My son=my life
My Heart Flows
He=My Husband
After You
Love Attack
Hoping for a Lifetime
My King
Love Advantage
Not Taken for Granted
To the One
You Give me
Undeniable Feeling
Us 2

## Pain & Hurt..........................................................................17
April 1st (2000)
Dear mane Mane
My Cry
Tired of Lies
I should be used to this
Again
When will it rain?
Look for a way out

## Focus & Healing...................................................................27
Vengence is not mine!
Fragments
How
My mind is tainted
Swan
What do you see in me?
Remember when

Letting you go!
STOP
If you opened the door
Away with depression/stressing
Thank God You're Gone
Recovery
Too attached to God
Goals
Permission Granted
What you do for Christ will last

**Prayer**............................................................................................46

Thank you for introducing me
Coming to you
Sin and Life
God Blessed You
I thought...
Not giving up on you
Sometimes/Some things
Faith without works
In due time
God hear me
So Bold
How I pray
Thank you Lord
If I Could
Prayer Poem


*BONUS Poems*......................................................................65
*Excerpt from the book Take Pain and Walk:*
*Short Stories I Never Told*...................................................72

# LOVE

Photo by Leighann Renee on Unsplash

## To Loron M. Young

They tried to write you off
Before you were born
In the world the enemy
Tried to scorn
Rosemary's baby is what
One called you
NO!!! My lil king, my mook mook
Me and your Dad had so many fights
While pregnant, he tried to push me
Downstairs,
Exactly one flight.
He had to go,
He just don't even know.
Where he put the bags down,
God picked them up
And blessed us with so much stuff.
He takes care of us
Not no hood nigga that
Runs the streets
It's God you cannot beat.
You may not have an earthly father,
But you have a Father in Heaven,
Lorenzo don't even bother.

I pray some man to complete our family,
Please believe he will have to be
A Christian down to a "T"
Son of Satan?
No. the fight was too hard,
Loron is the son of God

2006

# My son = my life

My son is my life
He knows no pain or strife
No cares of the world
My son = my fight
With this world daily,
No ifs, and's, or maybes
Teaching him what's right
Training him the true light
Learning from me to work for his
But he's still busy being a kid
My heart he will always have
Don't want him to grow up too fast
My son is my blessing from God
My wakeup call and why I work hard
One day he will be a man of his own
But that's not until he is grown
My son = My Life

Loron M. Young

August 2014

Proverbs 22:6 (KJV)
Train up a child in the way he should go: and when he is old,
he will not depart from it.

## My heart flows

Once my mind is made up
Then I had enough
All I wanted was some attention
and that's what's up
Can I have a little of your time?
Expand what's on your mind.
Trying to get your heart closer to mine,
Temptation is a thin line
A good morning text would be fine
A call good night before I lay in bed inclines
A lil intimacy
I thought one day we will be
My heart flows gracefully
For you

March 2015

## He=My Husband

He is what I am not
My strength in my weak spot
He takes care of his wife and home
Even a seed that's not his own
He speaks full of substance
Having my attention in an instance
He helps me feel safe and secure
Lord knows I've waited
And time for me to endure
He has amazing, bold faith
A Christian saved by Grace
God has blessed me
with desires of my heart
And giving us, our family,
a beautiful start
Remember to love me, your wife
As you love your own body, for life
Reverenced, appreciated, and loved
Daily thanking the One up above

December 30, 2010

Ephesians 5:28-31 (KJV)
So ought men to love their wives as their own bodies. He that loveth his wife loveth himself. For no man ever yet hated his own flesh; but nourisheth and cherisheth it, even as the Lord the church: For we are members of his body, of his flesh, and of his bones.
For this cause shall a man leave his father and mother, and shall be joined unto his wife, and they two shall be one flesh.

*After you*

No one I would rather wait for,
but you I adore.
No one I would rather chase after,
but you give my heart laughter.
For you I would wait
and for you I would chase,
we need no space
Between us.
There is a future and a reason,
let's take advantage of our season.
To see you and smile,
happiness when I pick up and dial.
Feel protected, safe confident
and comfortable with you.
Dare not to think of possibility
of not having you
Crazy at the thought
but I'm after you.

## Love Attack

Sometimes I get wrapped up in fear,
cause this what we have,
is different my dear.
Unexplainable explosive feeling,
when love loves you back
Man, it's like a dream
caught up in a Love-Attack
I don't want any away time,
that's when my thoughts
get out of line
But you bring me
back to my senses.
One look at you,
relieve tensions

January 30, 2013

# Hoping for a Lifetime

People come into your life
For a reason, season, or a lifetime
After months in, I feel like God
threw me a lifeline
I thank God for you every day,
honestly, I look at you
and don't know what to say
My true feelings
but God Knows my heart
I don't want to mess up cause,
I feel this is a brand-new start
Hope you're here for more than a season,
I think I understand God's reason
Hope it's for a lifetime,
you stay in my dreams
and stay on my mind
I fell in love by mistake
but my feelings I can't shake
God has a plan but hoping
you're my true man
One day I'll be able to share my feelings
But for now,
I'll just enjoy the view

## My King

You're the one that's been around
Through thick and thin,
You've seen my ups and downs.
So thankful to have you by my side,
Thankful to share this ride.
Been together with nothing,
Watching the blessings
unfolding to something.
Blessed to have you in my life,
What we have together
no man can bring us strife,
I appreciate you
and you loving me,
Together I hope
we will always be.
Soon we will be doing our thing,
So proud this Queen has a King

February 15, 2015

## Love Advantage

Taking advantage of your love,
Feel like heaven opened up above.
You are a true man,
when I can't, you can.
Thanks for having my back,
I definitely like that.
You put a smile on my face,
you are the one,
my ace no one can replace.
Time spent on us,
Unforgettable moments,
and nothing to fuss.
I'm enjoying our times,
just as I enjoy writing you these lines.
I have endured much pain,
joy, and happiness, you bring.
I deserve it all!
Your love I gladly to fall

## Not Taken for Granted

I don't take you for granted,
you have me like an addict.
Blown away on how I'm treated
day by day.
Love is an expression
that can't be told
but powerful enough
for people to experience is bold
Action speaks louder than words.
Your look, touch, and the way
you feel my curves.
Never a doubt that I love you
You're a keeper,
my best kept secret.

January 10, 2013

## To the one

Hmmm where do I start?
...To the one that captured my heart...
A real woman recognizes a real man
In my eyes,
My secret superman
hard worker, humorous, achiever,
A man with goals,
Can't wait to talk or see you,
And don't like to see you go.
Thanks for encouraging me,
and asking about my day.
You're awesome and appreciated,
is all I can say.
Thanks for making me smile,
Thanks for the laughs.
I was skeptical at first,
But glad we crossed paths.
If I had the opportunity,
we would be more than friends.
To the one that captured my heart
Much love for ya'
The End

August 4, 2012

You give me

Somebody to miss
Somebody to kiss
A person to appreciate
That person
reciprocates
You to desire
Me, you inspire
Communication in sharing
Gratification in caring
Thoughtful you are
My gratefulness by far

January 14, 2013

## Undeniable Feeling

Feeling an undeniable thing,
more than what a new year can bring,
Freshness, greatness, and awesome all over,
like joy in finding a 4-leaf clover
But this is not luck.
Love is indescribable,
and the feeling is undeniable
Thankful that everything
has something good to come out,
God has definitely showed out
"I" the question and "he" the answer,
Love has a way of feeling pampered
Genuine trust and honesty,
Thanking God as love can be
Love is real,
God gave me the best deal
This testimony I keep in my heart
Accepted by those who believe in love,
we fit together like a glove and
Daily thanking the heavenly Father above.

January 14, 2013

## Us 2

You were helping me
clean up my mess
In the process
you were helping me destress
Didn't realize you were the one
and had my back,
one day writing a poem
about a Love-attack
Unknowingly came together,
My friend plus my man
is the best thing ever
Sitting here missing you
Reminiscing about us 2

# PAIN & HURT

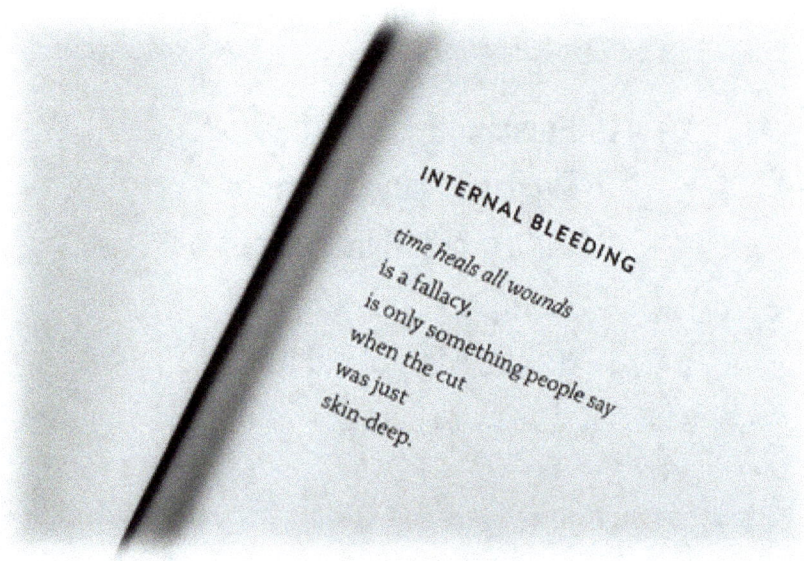

Photo by Thought Catalog on Unsplash

## April 1st (2000)

Upset cause you're not with me
Things shift so swiftly
I remember that day
I'm praying to keep the evil away
I'm mad that you're gone
The family continues to hold on
My heart dropped when I heard you died
I lost count on how many times I cried
That idiot just don't know what he did
I wanted to put two in his head
He didn't know what he was doing
Or whose life he ruined
I seen your baby girl
She don't even know
She's missing half of the world
Your soul lives through us
We'll never forget April 1st
We'll all be together again,
Our fam and Mane Mane
Once again you still live on
Through us, the family, and this poem
From your Detroit cousin Lise,
May you Rest In Peace

April 1, 2001

## Dear Mane Mane

I apologize for not visiting your grave
On Father's Day,
My mind was still in disarray,
Honestly, I can never lie
That day I almost cried
When I saw Earnesha,
And saw you in her eyes
I wish you were still here,
So, I wouldn't shed a tear.
I hung out with our other cousins,
But it feels incomplete,
I'll try not to worry,
Cause we're all going to meet.
We're still upset that you're gone,
But we're keeping our heads up
To continue on.
For those niggas who murdered you
I feel sorry for them too.

Because if they are in the family's presence
We're going to make Hell their
Permanent residence.
Mane Mane continue to
Rest in Peace
Save us a spot in Heaven
For your family
Love your cousin, Lise

## My Cry

I can feel it I can touch it,
it's built up in my soul.
Someone tell me
how to let it go?
This hurt this pain it's all familiar
and it's all the same.
You can't ignore it.
People have to endure it.
Clutter in my brain
teardrops leave a stain.
Something I gotta change......
but His name remains da same
His love is for us all.
It's time I give Him a call.
Jesus, I need your help
I turn to no one else.
Please I need you now;
these tears won't stop falling down,
Hear me, help me
YOU all I've got
My Cry...
Pray with me
Amen

June 30, 2011

# Tired of lies

I'm tired of the lies
Let's push the bullsh\*\*t aside
I just wanna know why
Deep down I'm hurting inside
Hurt so bad I can't even cry
I'm tired of your lies
Hurting again
I'm trying to amend
You keep cutting the knots
I keep sewing it together
This thing was meant forever
What happened to us?
All over again
Only you have been tempted to sin
Only the devil comes to steal kill destroy
I can't take it anymore
Praying behind these doors
Waiting for my expected end
I just want you back

May 5, 2011

## I should be used to this

Always been your cheerleader,
I wanted to be a fearless leader.
Maybe you're not used to this,
I could write books on this.
Back to a familiar place,
Where I was anxious and couldn't wait.
Sitting around waiting with life,
All I wanted was to be a wife.
Dreams keep on dreaming,
You left, and I guess
it took a different meaning.
Encouraged you to the fullest,
How it seems I'm so foolish.
How could I do this again,
My baby boy, now, ten,
no nearest next of kin.
Sitting, writing, questioning God,
What's the lesson in this?
Guess I am letting go,
My faith always exist,
But with man, it diminishes.
Man, I should be used to this.

March 15, 2015

## Again

My heart is in surgery again
Gave my heart to someone I thought
Was more than a friend
Dude just abused it,
dropped it,
And broke it again
But God is always there
To repair and amend
The ultimate surgeon
That's listening again
Forgiving my faults
Cause I'm a mere human
Understanding, listening, and directing
Me at 2 in the morning
God thanks for doing
This for me again and again

James 5:16 (NIV)
Therefore confess your sins to each other and pray for each other so that you may be healed. The prayer of a righteous person is powerful and effective.

July 5, 2010

## When will it rain?

These thoughts stay on my brain
Wondering when…. will…it…. rain
In captivated with pain
But I am coming for what I came
Trying to make everything a gain
Wondering when…. will…it…. rain
These seeds I've sewn
These thoughts only grown
My plans I make to you are known
Looking to see if I should dip and get gone
Wondering when…. will…it…. rain
Seeking you for help
Using what I have left
Almost feels like petty theft
Then I think,
I am blessed
Bring the rain

## Looking for a way-out

So emotionally confused,
I thought I paid my dues,
Set up to win
then lose.
Been a long time coming,
this fool keep fronting.
When I think it's right,
I'm totally wrong.
I can't keep going on,
Different man, same song.
I have nothing to stand on,
so its best I am gone.
Loyal to the end,
need no new friends,
In God I trust

March 5, 2016

# FOCUS & HEALING

Photo by Jeremy Yap on Unsplash

## Vengeance is not mine!

I know what I said
I would've put 2 in their heads
But you have
to understand
I was very angry back then
But God showed up
And showed me his marvelous light
HE wiped all the tears away
That I used to cry at night
HE delivered you into your enemy's hands
That's God, it's His will, He can
They will still have to pay
I hope they repent and pray
Vengeance is not mine,
Nor yours,
It's the Lord's!

May 10, 2006

Romans 12:19 (KJV)
Dearly beloved avenge not yourselves but rather give place unto
wrath: for it is written, Vengeance is Mine; I will repay saith the Lord

# Fragments

I'm not talking in complete sentences
Nothing is making sense
When is this going to give?
God, I just want to live
My mind is confused
and what shall I do
But I only cry to you
You are the only one
that understands
With everyone else
I throw up my hands
Man can be so ridiculous
Sometimes making me repetitious
God, you are tremendous
More than enough
Comfort my heart and troubles
No matter where I go

Psalm 77

# How

How do I keep praying
and staying ahead?
I want perpetual growth
but sin in my bed.
I love this man dearly,
but I question myself,
God how can I sin
and ask for your help?
How do I make this right?
How can I fully trust
and get rid of this feeling in my gut?
When I'm not sure,
I need you to step in.
I need to control my emotions,
so you can amend.

My mind is tainted

My mind is tainted
Painted with this life I
Wanted to leave
Old thoughts have risen
My mind is a prison
Gotta get back to work and
Keep my mind occupied
Stinking thinking
Keep me sinking
But God is calling me higher
Because much is required of
Me and of thee

October 14, 2009

## Swan

Even the ugly
duckling turned
To a swan
Then to be with
She had to find the one
God never meant for man
To be alone
That's why He took
From man's bone
So, he would have a help
Mate for his home
He that findeth a wife
Findeth a good thing
This swan is waiting
for the right
Man, to cling.
A king

July 2, 2010

What do you see in me?

Is it the car, my job, the raise?
This is only a few things
of why I praise!
He knows what you need,
Ask and you shall receive.
Can't buy what I have,
Go to Him and steadfast
Took some trash and cleaned it up
and made it brand new
You're wondering what you see,
how could it happen to you?
I'm not an overnight success,
Pain, suffering, and wondering,
This is a lifetime process.
Can't you see, He is still
working on me.
Greater is He, that is in me that is in the world,
Is what you see

Remember when

I used to drink so much
I couldn't think
I smoked weed that
I forgot importance
of my seed my kids
I did drugs
I forgot where I was
Sex, drugs, money,
had me missing for days.
Do you remember when?
I skipped school being a fool.
Remember I used to fight,
staying up with you
and arguing all night.
Remember when I got saved?
How God touched my life,
I started doing things that were right
I left Satan's kingdom,
advanced to God's freedom
If He can save a wretch like me
I feel a change you can see
I started a relationship with God
Go and sin no more

## Letting you go!

I was killing myself
I didn't even know
You guys keep taking
and penetrating
I had to let you go.
Alcohol, sex, marijuana,
I only did it
when I was down
Feelings, emotions, of hope
Of being with you.
I had to let you go.
Disrespect, anger, unclean things,
Wasting time with the same scenario,
I had to let you go.
Because God was calling, tugging
And pulling me.
HE captured my heart
This was my brand-new start.
I let go
To lose and to gain.
I had to grab a hold of Jesus
It's the devil's kingdom
I had to let go!

# STOP

Stressed as I put to rest
all these pains I have inside
Sorrowful becomes too powerful
as I cry on the outside
Blame all the pain
that I seem to go insane in the brain
Stop all the fuss I feel
as I'm about to cuss
Ball of confusion
stop all this losing
when will I begin to win?
so, I turn to You
Only you can undo
the hurt, pain
numbness that I feel.
God, what can I do?
this is surreal,
Seems like I was on top,
But God can you make
these emotions stop.

## If you opened the door

If you would've opened the door
Could you imagine the life
we could've explored?
Who could've knew,
a life of me and you?
Maybe you could've made
my dreams come true
Temptation may have been
something you couldn't resist
Or dreams of a tender kiss
You may have been mine
and you could cancel
all your player lines
Memories of arising situation
thoughts of existing contemplation
But you didn't open the door
Now we will never know

## Away with depression/stressing

Moving around to have to constantly adjust
Life's so demanding,
it's almost a must
I thrust for understanding
It's like a step back.
what I seek you lack,
What God sees through these eyes,
At night He hears my cries
Feeling all men lie
My soul needs to die
Always left standing strong
No more friends and foes
Never the one to jump on the bus,
No longer have to fight and fuss.
It's time to catch up,
Plan on leaving you in the dust.
My heart feels ashamed,
My heart has had pain.
Disregard the lame.
As we grow older,
Life isn't the same.

Looking out for help.
Everyone for self
They say it was all pride,
Now that I can't deny
No longer seem helpless
It's God the one that Blesses
I pray He takes all my stress
No more all-day headaches
No more lifelong heartbreaks
My Lexus stops here
No time to fear
Time to move on,
I pray I keep strong

## Thank God you're gone

Thank God that you're gone
I don't have to write
no more of these sad poems.
Feels good to be free,
just getting to know me.
Feels like heaven
You came, and I went,
Don't have to stay bent.
Money, I lent,
and I stayed
so you could get laid
Not no more,
not your personal whore.

## Recovery

Needing mouth-to-mouth recovery
Chest compressions
Bring me back to life as soon as can be
Run the I.V. through my veins,
living life just isn't the same
God allow me to breathe
I need a breath of fresh air
Smothered by the confusion
of how to get there
Really just wipe my eyes
and hold me tight
Sometimes I need to hear,
it's going to be all right
An answer needed
have my decisions lacking oxygen
About to pass out
from lack of confidence
Inject me with some optimism,
Defeat the syndrome of the opposition
Comfort in knowing
who holds tomorrow
Please God hide me, until you revive me
Full and complete recovery is what I need

## Too Attached to God

I'm growing so attached to you
I'm doing things that I shouldn't do
But hopefully, God blesses you
Greater is HE that is in you than he
That is in the in the world
I'm just a city girl
Trying to shine the light of God's world
Hope you see his marvelous light
He has the strength, the power, and the might
I am too attached to God to go astray
So daily, for you, I pray
That God continues to bless you
And you to do his will
And may the Holy Spirit guide
And keep you filled

John 8:12 (NIV)
When Jesus spoke again to the people, he said, "I am the light of the world. Whoever follows me will never walk in darkness, but will have the light of life.

1 John 4:4 (NIV)
You, dear children, are from God and have overcome them because the one who is in you is greater than the one who is in the world.

## Goals

Goals sitting right next to me
Job getting the best of me
Give me my moment
I bet you'll see
Looking for a way out
Trying to show myself
what I'm all about
Put my goals out of reach
but I came back
put in the back seat
But now my focus
is greater than

## Permission Granted

Hook the cables to my heart
Had to give my life
another jump start
They may have thought
my life was dead
Could no longer drag
and begin to dread
Prayed to God
and He gave me the go-ahead
Going in no stopping,
foot on the gas
As He grants me a pass
God told me to go ahead
and do what I showed you
My thoughts, deepest dreams,
utilizing everything by any means

## What you Do for Christ will Last

What you do for Christ will last
Whether you sing or dance
What you do for Christ will last
Whether you rap to a beat
And Move our feet
What you do for Christ will last
Slow or fast I listen to you
To guide me through
What you say I do
For Christ will last
Poetry or mime ministry
Bad times will past
However, what you do for Christ
Will last

# PRAYER

Photo by Alex Woods on Unsplash

Thank you for introducing me

You desired to be loved
Materials required
I gave you a man, dog, cat
But you forgot the one above
Thank you for introducing me
The One that doesn't have to
result in seducing me
You can call on Him any time
He never has a busy line
He has a plan and peace for us
There's nobody like Jesus
HE guides me He leads me
He directs my path,
thank you for showing me something
I already had


Matthew 6:33 (KJV)
But Seek ye first the kingdom of God, and his righteousness; and all these things shall be added unto you.

## Coming to You

Lord, I don't know
where to start
Suppose to have
a forgiving heart
Sometimes this seems a little hard
My life is a lil scarred
I pray so I won't fall apart
Tell me why people lie
That's a hurtful
feeling inside
To you, I tell and cry
But my tears you always dry
Praise the Lord Jesus Christ

## Sin and Life

Sin is free
But life is priceless
When it's all said and done
I want to be
Where Christ is
Who are those that are sinless?
Continually ask for forgiveness
We all fall short
We each have a report
We all have a story
God-given testimony
But it is He that gets all the Glory
For the righteousness will never be forsaken
Turn from sin and accept God
The gift of eternal life is for the taking.

December 25, 2010

Romans 6:23 (KJV)
For the wages of sin is death; but the gift of God
is eternal life through Jesus Christ our Lord.

## God Blessed You

The devil can't mess with you
No matter what his flock may do
Keep standing tall
You rise, they fall
As usual, the devil is mad
We're blessed and highly favored
And I'm glad
Everything that happened is not your fault
Don't look back
you may turn into a pillar of salt
Keep the sunshine flowing
Through his eternal bloodline,
keep it going
Don't let anything stop you
Because the devil can't mess with you

## I thought...

I thought I lost you
When you told me
You have cancer,
Back spasms and bronco spasms
I thought I lost you
When I heard you lost your job,
had no place to live,
They were going to take your kids.
I thought I lost it
Lost my man, lost friends
God literally grabbed you
Truthfully always had you
Incline your ear, because
God's always near
God has blessed you,
So, we should never fear

Not giving up on you

Lord I tried,
my feelings I can't deny
I have some pain
and hurt inside,
trying to mask my pride
This time I didn't cry
Only thing I can do is sigh
I'm calling you God
because you are nigh
I believe in you, not in man
Please bring my man
Back safely and
quickly as you can

## Sometimes/Some things

Guess I'll start writing again
Only things I need is paper and pen
Sometimes I feel like
God is my only friend
Sometimes I feel like
Things I can't grasp in my hand
Some things only God can amend
Some things I just don't want to let go
Sometimes I feel like my heart don't flow
Sometimes I feel like I just don't know
Then I remember it's God I never let go.

July 22, 2012

Philippians 3:13-14 (KJV)
13 Brethren, I count not myself to have apprehended: but
this one thing I do, forgetting those things which are behind,
and reaching forth unto those things which are before,
14 I press toward the mark for the prize of the high calling of
God in Christ Jesus.

## Faith without works

Faith without works is Dead
Go to work like the Detroit Pistons
Is what Pastor Davis Said
Don't put your faith in man "Ah Man"
One of Sis Davis Encourage-A-Sister's topics
Let God work, you in his master plan.
You have to have somewhere to start,
Believe have faith, God knows your heart.
Seek God first, lean not to your own understanding,
He will start to open the floodgates of Heaven.


Heb 11:1 (KJV)
Now faith is the substance of things hoped for, the evidence of things not seen.

James 2:17 (KJV)
Even so faith, if it hath not works, is dead, being alone.

## In due time

Memories suppressed
come back to my mind
These thoughts are way out of line
Running out of time
A little behind
His word says in due time
A decision to follow you
No matter what life
Puts me through
Every day you're on my mind
Even when I get out of line
Remember His word says
In due time

## God Hear Me

I'm tired I'm fed up
this ain't where I wanna be
I hear God saying just come to me
I feel like people blocking my blessings
Wait a minute, that's me, I'm stressing
Holding my tongue, holding my peace,
God this ain't where I want to be!
I work, take responsibility, I have 2 college degrees,
But here I am taking mess from all the wanna BE's
I keep pressing toward the mark of your high calling
But your people keep pushing me to keep falling
I need your help your direction,
Your voice Your peace Your protection
Lead me to where you want me to be
I hear you calling me, but they have my ears clogged
Sometimes I can't see through this thick fog
God what is it that you want me to do!
I tried to please people
YOU are the only One who can help me pull through
So, I'm calling you while you are nigh
God help me to continue to do what's right

October 8, 2010

2 Corinthians 4: 17-18 (KJV)

17- For our light affliction, which is but for a moment, worketh for us a far more exceeding and eternal weight of glory.

18- While we look not at the things which are seen, but at the things which are not seen: for the things which are seen are temporal; but the things which are not are eternal.

## So Bold

I ask myself
How are you so bold?
But I know how grace
Let's it unfold
I keep it to pen and paper
Let His truth be told
Can't keep it to myself
But sometimes get hold

## How I Pray

Hoping God hearing me
Cause my mind deceiving me
On my knees is where I be
My head bowed unto He
Focused on things, I cannot see
My eyes are yet tearfully
Your strength is what I need
My palms together prayerfully
My mouth praises thee
Asking you to show me
Don't care how tired I be
Hoping God hearing me

February 21, 2011

## Thank You Lord

When dude put a gun to my head,
I thought I was dead,
But listen to what I said;
Thank you, Lord...
For keeping me covered
To the crown of my head
to the soles of my feet,
without you the enemy
I couldn't defeat
Thank you, Lord....
When my marriage went south
In self, I had all doubt.
As smoking and drinking weren't enough,
I quit but PCOS is tough.
Thank you for keeping me filled
It was you that increased my skills
Thankful for getting back on my feet
Without you, I'm not complete
The devil took everything, and you
Gave it all back plus more
No matter what I've been through
God is who I turn to.
Ear to hear. Faith without works.
Show you my faith by my work!

## If I Could

Man let me tell you how I feel
Why you rob, steal, and kill?
Taking a full-course meal
Playing relationships like monopoly
How precious is a family?
How deceiving you can be.
This world is not yours.
Having sons and daughter disobey orders.
So, their lives on this earth can be shorter.
You're the crack in the foundation,
God allowed you since creation.
My knees to the floor
Praying so you can't creep in no more
You try to destroy many lives
But you fail to realize
God is over all
He rises when we fall

## Prayer Poem

Enter my body Lord
And cleanse me out
Give me knowledge, so I know
What you're all about
Wrap me with your
Presence Lord
And keep me safe
Take over my mind
Fill me
Cleanse me
Wrap me
Help me
Work me
Accept me
Love me
Understand me
Release me
Comfort me
Peace be with me
Reject the enemy
God I continually seek thee

Psalms 121:1(KJV)
I will lift up mine eyes unto the hills, from whence cometh my help.

# BONUS POEMS ©

## PCOS Accepted

We laugh, we cry
We seem to don't know why
We finally accept it
Either fight or get rejected
Do what's right, do what's best,
But Cyster, try not to stress
Continue to push through,
be proud of this ribbon, teal blue
Your PCOS Cyster, Love you

As far back as I can remember, I have always been told by doctors I had a hormonal disorder. After I had my son, a doctor diagnosed me with Polycystic Ovary Syndrome (PCOS). I became enlightened that this condition has a name but it's a constant struggle. No worries, I got this!

## Someone Like You #2 (2003)

You were a smooth a\*\* trick,
Thought you had me hooked on your d\*ck.
You got yours and had to get gone,
I was left with no explanation and still alone.
One thought I remember, we had a good time
but I find it hard to erase you from my mind.
I have a new oath, promise #2
NOT to dare or even speak to you.
It seems no one understands,
I got my heart broken again,
to someone who had potential
of being my man.
I was too well prepared,
And it seemed like he was scared.
I'm trying to get over it, It's ok, hopefully
I'll have a man someday.
It was a nice costume before I tore it off!
I found out you were fake,
you should be an actor or a costume director.
You trick a\*\* snake.
I knew it was too good to be true,
for me to end up with someone like you.

## AIN'T NOT GREATER LOVE

Ain't no love greater than
the fun we have
Ain't no love expression that
this pen and pad
Aint not love thought, of thoughts
I've ever had
Ain't no love greater than what has
formed in my mind
Ain't no love greater than that
comes with time
Ain't no love greater than
A Love-Attack
Ain't no Love greater than
having each other back
Ain't no love greater than
you and me
Ain't no love greater than
the love we have
You changed my thoughts to love again and again
To the love of my life, my man, and my best friend
Shaun Walker, may we express our love, over time
until the end.  Love Lise

7/20/2014

Without using his hands

He gives me a natural high
Every time he walks by
I peek out the corner of my eye
At the same time,
I can't contain
As I look back
glad we became
more than friends
I fell in love with the way he
touches me
without using his hands


Song of Solomon 3:4 (part of)
I have found the one whom my soul loves

7/6/2021

## Tough Conversations

I admit I avoid tough conversations
To avoid confrontation
My mind contemplating
On the next situation
The outcome probably bad
In the end, we both mad
Overall, we said what we said
We all got it out of our heads.
Now excuse me, I apologize
This right conversation is not meant
to hurt you or make you cry
only realize a different side
We are not always right and
we don't have to fight
just to see others' perspectives
It was my only objective.
Sometimes I choose not to contemplate
So, I'd rather walk away
To avoid confrontation

5/17/2021

## Only A Fan—Aaliyah

It felt as if you were close to my heart,
I'm so messed up; I don't know where to start.
I'm only a fan
And still don't understand.
I can't look at a poster or picture.
You don't know how bad I miss ya.
So devastating and close at hand
but I'm only a fan
It's the same feeling as April 1st
When my cousin died, it's the same, it hurts.
You were so successful and great in every show
But I was a fan you didn't know.
Vicky and Grace told me you went to a better place.
The one with the Golden Gates
The place we're all trying to reach, Heaven,
You're with my Grandma, Grandpas, and cousin.
I'm still heartbroken because you are gone
That's why I wrote this poem.
But I'm only a fan
Saddened with disbelief and I don't understand.
I'm just a fan who wrote you a poem
One of my #1 R&B singers, Aaliyah,
your soul lives on
From your Detroit Fan Lise
May you Rest in Peace

9/1/2001

# Excerpt From
# Take Pain and Walk:
# Stories I Never Told
# -Short Stories and Poems-

# Take Pain and Walk: Stories I Never Told ©

## 11850 Engleside

Growing up, my parent's room seemed to be sacred. We didn't just go in there unannounced or just sat in their room. My parents were separated and divorced in the 90s. As I became an adult living with my mother, I still held those standards about her room. This time around, her room became my safe haven.

The first time he jumped on me, I felt like it was just a fight I lost. In my mind back then, it was not abuse but I was pregnant. I still lived with my mother. The first time, he got mad because I wouldn't give him my last $5 to buy him some "loosies". Loose cigarettes. "No, that's all I got", I said. I was sitting up in the bed. Don't remember much, just arguing. Then he started shoving me around and backing me in a corner. We were in the house alone, upstairs. We both pulled and tugged, and I kept protecting my stomach. We got to the top of the stairs.

He tried to push me down those stairs, exactly one flight. I caught myself. Glad I didn't fall down those 17 steps of hardwood. I ran down. He eventually left.

The next time we got into a fight I vaguely remember what it was for. I ran to the kitchen, and I fell to the floor. I remember protecting my stomach again. This time I felt a fist in my face. I don't know how but I got up and ran into my mother's bedroom and locked the door.

My mother had a landline phone in her room. I quickly dialed my oldest sister's phone number. I tried to hurry up and tell her what was going on because Lawrence was trying to bust the door open. Lawrence busts through the door and snatches the phone, and the phone cord out the wall. Tussling, I broke free again. This time he leaves with a frantic look in his eyes as he hustles out the side door. I heard the front door and my other sister. Not the oldest one I called but the one close to my age.

My oldest sister must have called her. Someone called 911 because the police showed up too. My sister who came started crying as she saw the black eye and the blood coming from my nose. The police officer asks questions, two I remember. Do you have any children? I stated, "No, but I am five months pregnant". The second question was do you want to press charges? Regretfully I delayed my response, looked at my sister, and still said "No". I knew it would be hard for them to find him because he is unstable and at the same time, I didn't want anything bad to happen to the father of my child.

Lawrence was the nicest human being when around people. By ourselves, he was totally different. He flipped out on me when he didn't get what he wanted. He stole material things like my CDs and DVDs but never stole any money I had. I thought to myself once, Is this nigga on drugs? I mean I knew he smoked weed but maybe 51's. What we called it coming up, was weed mixed with Angel dust (cocaine).

## Narcissist Transference

I think the lowest of my lowest
When he said I didn't need no friends
Messed up part I believed him
Like we had future plans
He told me all I needed was him
Fed me with a bunch of lies
I was blinded by his narcissistic disguise
Mental fog of brainwashing
Young, I believed him even
when I couldn't get through
Dr. Jekyll and Mr. Hyde
To my surprise when
he blackened my eye
I kept to myself, trusted no one
Hide and seek from everyone
I finally found the strength of no more.
As God as my witness,
my son and I out the door.

I may not talk to certain people who have wronged me. I have tried to talk to a few that may have rejected my welcome. I may never get an apology. It's cool, I've come to terms that I've repented and forgave, yet didn't forget because it's a part of my testimony. Today I realize that as long as they go to the Lord ask for forgiveness and repent, that is what really matters. Your relationship with God is better than a relationship with me. We all heal differently; doesn't mean you are allowed back in my personal space. You can forgive without reconciling

www.ingramcontent.com/pod-product-compliance
Lightning Source LLC
Chambersburg PA
CBHW051309060526
44119CB00102B/429/J